A Great Big Welcome
by Robin Mercer
Perfect for hanging across the front of the house or driveway, this big greeting makes yours the most notable house on the block and helps your guests find the party.

MATERIALS - size 16" x 75":
Paper Accents chipboard pennants (2-Point: seven 8" x 12", seven 10" x 16") • Decorative papers • 6" tall letters (Black, White) • Rhinestone (Glue strips, Embellishments) • 6 yards ribbon • Glitter • Pop Dots adhesive • White glue • *Xyron* adhesive

Small Welcome
A small banner fits anywhere... even folded in an envelope.

MATERIALS - size 8" x 40":
Paper Accents chipboard pennants (2-Point: seven 4" x 6", seven 6" x 9") • Decorative papers • 6" tall letters (Black, White) • Rhinestone glue strips and embellishments • 8 ribbons, each 80" long • Glitter • Pop Dots adhesive • White glue • *Xyron* adhesive

INSTRUCTIONS FOR BIG AND SMALL WELCOME:
Cover chipboard shapes with papers. Use Pop Dots to adhere small chipboard to large. Adhere rhinestones. Use a Xyron to apply adhesive to the front side of the White letters. Cover with fine glitter. Tap off excess. Adhere White glitter letters to Black letters creating a drop shadow with Black. Attach letters to chipboard shapes. Run ribbon through holes, center and knot the ends.

Whether it is small or large, your banner will be a welcome addition to any gathering or celebration.

Nostalgic Home
by Terry Olson
A serene color pallette and simple designs give this banner a calm appeal. This one's perfect for the den, study or family room.

MATERIALS:
Paper Accents chipboard pennants (2-Point: two 4" x 6", four 6" x 9") • Decorative papers • 2" tall paper letters • Paper die cuts (four 3" scallop circles, crown) • 2 glitter butterflies • Rhinestones • 2½ yards White twill ribbon • 2 yards 1½" wide wire edge ribbon • Pop Dots adhesive • White glue

INSTRUCTIONS - size 8" x 38":
Cover chipboard shapes with papers. Adhere letters to scallop circles. Attach circles and butterflies to pennants with Pop Dots. Adhere rhinestones. Run White twill ribbon through holes, center and knot the ends. Tie wired ribbon in bows between the large pennants.

Summer

by Aldean Tendick

It's Summer! Celebrate with a banner with the colors and motifs of your favorite season.

MATERIALS:
Paper Accents chipboard pennants (Triangle: eight 6" x 9") • Decorative papers • Cardstock • 1½" tall sparkly sticker letters • Colored brads, buttons • Flowers (Silk, paper) • Ribbon (2 yards Sheer, 8" Twill) • Die cut shapes • Word stickers • Scallop edge punch • Pop Dots adhesive • White glue • *Xyron* adhesive

INSTRUCTIONS - size 11" x 55":
Cover chipboard shapes with papers. Cut 8" x 11" cardstock into triangle shape and scallop the edges. Adhere chipboard to scallop edge backdrop. Attach embellishments and letters. Tie pennants together with ribbon.

Celebration

by Robin Mercer

Whether you are hosting a family reunion, birthday, graduation, or retirement party, this banner adds sparkle to your decor.

MATERIALS:
Paper Accents chipboard pennants (2-Point: seven 4" x 6") • Decorative papers • 18" each twill ribbon (Yellow, Green, Orange, Pink, Blue) • Glitter paint • White glue

INSTRUCTIONS -
size 6" x 32":
Cover chipboard shapes with papers. Run ribbon through holes, center and knot the ends.

America the Beautiful

by Robin Mercer

Patriotism isn't just for the 4th of July. This Americana banner looks attractive in your home all year long. Hang this one outside to welcome your serviceman or woman coming home on leave. For variety, change the phrase on the plaque and computer print it onto your paper. Here are a few ideas: God Bless America, Land of the Free Because of the Brave, Semper Fi, United We Stand, Liberty and Justice for All, One Nation Under God.

MATERIALS:
Paper Accents chipboard pennants (Rectangle Scallop: seven 6" x 9") • Decorative papers • Sticker letters and swirl • Paper flowers (4 different sizes for layering) • Embellishments • Glitter glue • 2 yards Blue ribbon • Pop Dots • White glue

INSTRUCTIONS - size 10" x 38":
Cut an 8" x 10" oval paper plaque from decorative paper. Apply "America the Beautiful" and swirl stickers. Cover chipboard shapes with papers. Adhere embellishments.
Adhere plaque to center pennant. Paint touches of glitter glue as desired. Run ribbon through holes, center and knot the ends.

Joy Banner

by Donna Goss
Joy and snowflakes naturally go together. Enjoy it all winter long.

MATERIALS:
Paper Accents chipboard pennants (Arched: three 5" x 8")
• Cardstock (Kraft, White)
• Decorative papers (Book page)
• 2 yards *Zipperstop* White $\frac{1}{2}$" wide seam binding • 6" x 30" White tulle • Glittered snowflake ornaments (three $6\frac{1}{2}$" x $6\frac{1}{2}$", three 1" x 1") • *Sizzix* (die cut machine, Tim Holtz Sizzlits Decorative strip Paper Rosette die) • *Inkadinkado* Snowflake stamp • *Hero Arts* Letter stamps • 9 Silver $\frac{3}{16}$" eyelets • 9 White 1" cardstock circles • *Ranger* (Adirondack Snowcap White pigment ink pad, Jet Black archival ink pad, Walnut Distress stain ink pad, ink blending tool, $\frac{1}{8}$" Wonder tape) • *We R Memory Keepers* Crop-a-dile • Sewing machine • Pencil • Scissors • PVA glue and glue brush • Hot glue gun, hot glue

Making Tulle Fringe
1. Fold tulle in half and then in half again. 2. Sew down one edge.

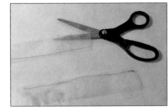

3. Cut open the fold on the opposite side of sewn edge. 4. Cut $\frac{1}{8}$" - $\frac{1}{4}$" fringe strips on un-sewn edge. Cut up to sewn edge but not through it.

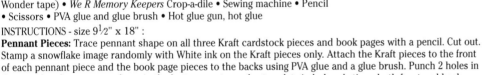

Kraft Cardstock Rosette
1. Die cut Kraft cardstock strip with rosette die in machine. Accordion fold die cut and tape ends together.

2. Bring top folds of rosette together and push down to form rosette. Place a 1" circle on the table. Hot glue the rosette to the circle.

INSTRUCTIONS - size $9\frac{1}{2}$" x 18" :

Pennant Pieces: Trace pennant shape on all three Kraft cardstock pieces and book pages with a pencil. Cut out. Stamp a snowflake image randomly with White ink on the Kraft pieces only. Attach the Kraft pieces to the front of each pennant piece and the book page pieces to the backs using PVA glue and a glue brush. Punch 2 holes in the top of each pennant and one in the bottom center and set eyelets in holes. Antique both front and back edges of pennants with Walnut ink and blending tool. Using the hot glue gun, attach large glittered snowflake ornaments to pennants. Tie small glittered snowflakes to bottom of each pennant through eyelet.

Making Rosette Pieces: Die cut rosettes from Kraft cardstock and book pages. Accordion fold die cut and tape ends together with Wonder tape. Die cut 3 spiked circles using Kraft cardstock. Stamp JOY letters on spiked circles in Black ink. Antique edges of spiked circles with Walnut ink and blending tool. Bring top folds of accordion folded diecuts together and push down to form rosettes. Using the hot glue gun attach the 1" White circles to the front and back centers of the book page rosettes and the backs only of the Kraft ones. Hot glue the Kraft stamped spiked circles to the front centers of the Kraft rosettes. Antique edges of Kraft rosettes only with Walnut ink and blending tool. Hot glue Kraft rosettes to the book page ones. Hot glue tulle fringe trim to back of book page rosettes. Layer once around and trim even at start.

Putting It All Together: Hot glue rosette layers to large glittered snowflakes on pennants. Tie pennants together with 12" ribbons. Knot securely. Tie 16" ribbons to outside eyelets on first and last pennants. Knot securely.

Noel

by Terry Olson
Sing Noel! Celebrate with a banner that captures the spirit of the season.

MATERIALS:
Paper Accents chipboard pennants (Concertina: four 8" x 12") • Decorative paper • Die cut letters 5" tall • Paper holly leaves • Paper flowers • Red ribbon $\frac{1}{4}$" wide • Rhinestone stickers • Four 1" buttons • $2\frac{1}{2}$ yards White twill ribbon • 35mm Silver jingle bell • Pliers • Hole punch • Pop Dots adhesive • White glue • Tape

INSTRUCTIONS - size 8" x 49":
Line up pennants so you can mark and punch holes at the bottom edges. Cover chipboard shapes with papers. Adhere letters. Join pennants together with lengths of chain. Attach jingle bell to each bottom chain with ribbon. Use the 1" button as a base and layer ribbon, holly leaves and flowers. Apply rhinestones to holly leaves.

Blessings
by Laurie Jacoby

Beautifully designed to complement an Autumnal season palette, Blessings will fit in with your Thanksgiving decor with an attractive reminder of why we celebrate the harvest.

MATERIALS:
Paper Accents chipboard pennants (Arched: nine 5" x 7", nine 4" x 6"; Glitz cardstock 12" x 12" Silver Midnight) • *ColorBox* Cat's Eye Bronze pigment ink pad • *Blue Moon Beads* (Angel Pendant metal wings, Metal Key Wing) • 2 yards Bronze sheer wire edge 1½" wide ribbon • Butterfly embellishment • Decorative paper • Paper die cut embellishments • *Making Memories* (Slice die cut machine, 3" tall letter dies) • Pop Dots • Glue • Tape
INSTRUCTIONS - size 7" x 52":
Cover chipboard with paper. Ink the edges. Tape small pennant to large. Die cut letters from Glitz cardstock and adhere with Pop Dots. Adhere embellishments. Tie pennants together with wired ribbon. Knot the ends.

Garden Garland
by Laurie Jacoby

This garland is a gardener's delight. It's perfect for the porch or wherever you sit to view your garden while planning the next flower bed or vegetable crop.

MATERIALS:
Paper Accents chipboard pennants (Arched: two 5" x 8", six 4" x 6"; Triangle: one 6" x 9") • Decorative papers • Rhinestone stickers • 5 yards twine • ½ yard raffia • Mushroom bird ornament • Buttons • Garden motif die cuts and embellishments • Scallop circle die cut letters 2" tall • 1½" circle punch • Mini Glue Dots • Glue • Tape runner
INSTRUCTIONS - size 10" x 36":
Cover pennants with paper. Adhere letters and embellishments to all small pennants and the last large one.
First Large Pennant, the Birdhouse - Punch 19 Brown circles to make the birdhouse roof. Place a 6" x 9" pennant under the arched pennants and position it so it supports the roof without showing. Lay the circles in layers over the supporting triangle to check the position. Trim the supporting triangle if needed and glue it to the back of the large arch. Adhere the circles to form roof tiles. Attach a scalloped circle to the center of the birdhouse for the door. Attach the bird and tie a bit of raffia to the bottom twig.
String pennants together with ribbon, tying bows between each pennant.
Secure bows in place with Glue Dots.

Cherry Pie Box
by Terry Olson

Pennant chipboard has a wide range of uses beyond banners. Create innovative and unique storage with boxes as delicious as pie.

MATERIALS:
Paper Accents chipboard pennants (Scallop Triangle: nine 4" x 6" for the top; Triangle: nine 4" x 6" for the bottom) • two 12" x 12" sheets of chipboard • Solid color 12" x 12" cardstock (2 Tan, 1 Dark Red, Matte Silver) • 2 sheets of adhesive Red glossy cardstock • Silver glitter • Pinking shears • *Xyron* Creatopia adhesive sheets • White glue • Double sided tape
INSTRUCTIONS - size of Pie:
   12" across, wedge: 4" x 6":
Prep: Apply an adhesive sheet to the back of Dark Red cardstock.

Pie Box - the Top
Weaving the Pie Top - Cut 2 sheets of Tan cardstock into ¾" wide strips using pinking shears. Smear glue on each edge and apply glitter. Weave Tan strips over the glossy side of Red glossy cardstock to create a pie top. Glue strips in place.

Pie Top - Box: Remove the adhesive covering from the back of Dark Red cardstock.. Place 9 Scallop edge pennants onto the adhesive for the pie top forming a circle. Cut around the shape. Cut out 2 sections for slices.

Pie Top - Crust Edge Reinforcement: Cut out 9 pieces of Tan cardstock, each 2" x 4½" for reinforcing the lid edge. Adhere 7 to the underside of the large lid edge for the large pie's edge, overlapping as needed. Set 2 aside for the lids to the two small Slices.

Pie Top - Crust Edge: Using the Scallop pennant edge as a template, cut Tan strips into scallops. Apply glitter. Adhere 7 pieces to the large pie's edge. Adhere the remaining 2 pieces to the pennants for the small Slice lids. Glue the edge reinforcement to the underside of each small Slice lid.

Pie Box and Slices: Cut 9 strips of Tan cardstock 1½" x 4½". Cut 9 chipboard strips 1½" x 4" and cut 6 chipboard strips 1½" x 5¾" for the box top and slices.

Large Box Sides: Tape 7 pieces of 4" strips together on the outside. The tape won't show because it will be covered with cardstock. Securely glue the sides to the top of the box, lining them up even with the edges. Cut 3 strips of Tan and 3 strips of Silver cardstock $1\frac{1}{2}$" x 12". Adhere Tan to the box, overlapping the ends. Cover with strips of Silver. Cut 1 strip of Red glossy cardstock $1\frac{1}{2}$" x 12" and adhere to the cut-out sides of the box.

Pie Box - the Bottom

Bottom of Large Box: Place a 12" x 12" sheet of chipboard on the table. Position 9 Triangle pennants on the chipboard square forming a pie. Trace the outer edge onto the 12" sheet. Remove 2 of the pennants and trace the edge of the cut out. Cut the 12" square on the lines. Adhere 7 pennants to the large chipboard. Be sure to leave a $\frac{1}{8}$" lip around the pennant edge.

Pie Slice Boxes

Note about the Slices: The top slice is just a bit larger than the bottom slice. This allows the bottom to fit inside of the top to make a small box.

Top of Slices: Use 2 of the $1\frac{1}{2}$" x 4" cardstock strips and 4 strips $1\frac{1}{2}$" x 6' long strips. Tape the pieces together on the outside. The tape won't show because it will be covered with cardstock. Glue one set to each of the woven Scallop Triangle pennants, lining them up even with the edges. Cut 2 strips of Tan cardstock $1\frac{1}{2}$" x 12". Adhere these to the Slice boxes, overlapping the ends. Cut 2 strips of glossy Red cardstock $1\frac{1}{2}$" x 12". Wrap a strip around the front of each Slice box.

Bottom of Slices: Cut 4 chipboard sides $1\frac{1}{2}$" x $5\frac{1}{2}$" and cut 2 Red cardstock sides $1\frac{1}{2}$" x 11". Cut 2 chipboard ends $1\frac{1}{2}$" x $3\frac{3}{4}$". Cut 2 Tan cardstock ends $1\frac{1}{2}$" x 8". Center the $1\frac{1}{2}$" x $3\frac{3}{4}$" chipboard end over the Tan $1\frac{1}{2}$" x 8" end and tape or glue together. Tape $5\frac{1}{2}$" strips at the point and to the Tan end flaps to form a triangle. Tape to a Triangle pennant bottom. Be sure to leave a $\frac{1}{8}$" lip around the pennant edge. Tape the sides to a Triangle pennant base. Cover the long sides with $1\frac{1}{2}$" x 12" Dark Red cardstock.

Pie Crust Edge

1. Use the Scallop Triangle pennant as a template to mark and cut the scallop edge slices of the box top.

 Use pinking shears to zig-zag cut the strips for the edges of the pie crust.

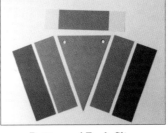

Bottom of Each Slice

2. For each Slice box bottom, use a Triangle pennant and cut 2 chipboard and 2 Red cardstock sides $1\frac{1}{2}$" x $5\frac{1}{2}$".

 Cut 1 chipboard end $1\frac{1}{2}$" x $3\frac{3}{4}$" and cut 1 Tan cardstock end $1\frac{1}{2}$" x 6".

3. Tape $5\frac{1}{2}$" pieces at the point. Tape to the Tan end flaps to form a triangle.

 Tape the triangle shaped edges to the Triangle pennant bottom.

 Be sure to leave a $\frac{1}{8}$" lip around the pennant edge.

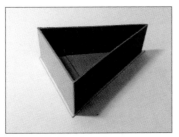

4. Cover the short side with a Tan strip. Cover the long sides with Dark Red strips of glossy cardstock.

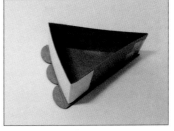

Top of Each Slice

5. Position a triangle on a Scallop pennant, lining up the edges evenly.

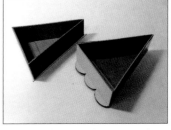

The Triangle bottom box is just a bit smaller than the top Scallop box. This allows a snug fit to make a small box.

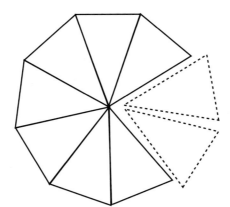

Diagram for pie bottom

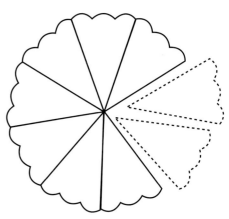

Diagram for pie top

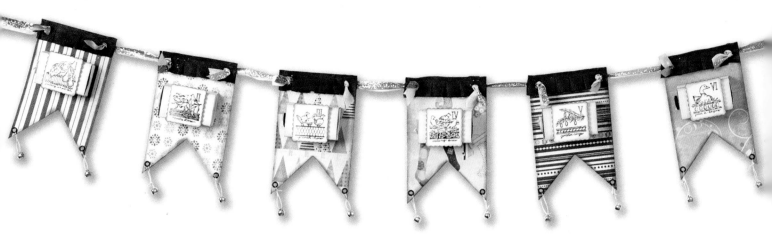

How to Emboss

1. Stamp image with pigment ink on Cream cardstock.

2. Pour embossing powder over image and shake off excess. Heat with a heat gun.

How to Make a Paper Drawer with a Button Pull

1. Die cut box bottom and lid.

2. Fold and glue the paper drawers. Punch s $\frac{1}{8}$" hole in the center of one end of the paper drawer.

3. Thread string through a white button then through hole in drawer from inside to outside. Pull button snug against drawer end.

4. Thread string through colored button and tie a knot snugly against the outside of the drawer.

Twelve Days of Christmas

by Donna Goss

Join the tradition of giving a gift on the 12 days of Christmas.

MATERIALS:
Paper Accents chipboard pennants (2-Point: twelve 4" x 6") • 12 sheets 12" x 12" decorative papers • 12 sheets each $8\frac{1}{2}$" x 11" solid cardstock (Yellow, Cream) • 55" Red 1" wide ruffle ribbon • String (24 pieces 8" Silver, 12 pieces 5" Cream) • *Zipperstop* Aqua seam binding (2 pieces $\frac{1}{2}$" x 20", 11 pieces $\frac{1}{2}$" x 12") • Aqua glitter ribbon (2 pieces $\frac{3}{8}$" x 20", 11 pieces $\frac{3}{8}$" x 12") • 48 Black $\frac{3}{16}$" eyelets • 24 Silver jingle bells • Buttons (12 White, 12 colored) • *Ranger* (Forest Moss Distress pad, Adirondack Pool paint dabber, Ink blending tool, Glossy Accents, Clear detail embossing powder) • *Clearsnap* Black pigment ink pad • *AccuCut* (die cutting machine, Matchbox die) • $1\frac{3}{4}$" scallop square punch • *Stampington & Co.* 12 days of Christmas stamps • $\frac{1}{8}$" hole punch • *We R Memory Keepers* Crop-a-dile • Heat gun • Pencil • Scissors • Hot glue gun • Hot glue • PVA glue and glue brush • Foam dots

INSTRUCTIONS - size 7" x 72":
Paint back and edges of pennants using Pool dabber. Let dry. Cover pennants with papers and ink the edges with Forest Moss. Hot glue ruffle ribbon to top of each pennant. Trim even at edges. Set eyelets in pennants at top and at each bottom point. Tie bells to pennant points with Silver string. From Yellow cardstock, die cut 12 match boxes and glue together. Ink edges with Forest Moss. Attach button pulls to one end of each drawer. Stamp and emboss images on Cream cardstock using Black ink and Clear detail powder. Punch out images with scallop square punch and ink the edges with Forest Moss and hot glue to match boxes. Hot glue match boxes to pennants. Tie pennants together with 12" ribbons. Knot securely. Tie 20" ribbons to outside eyelets on first and last pennants. Knot securely.

Fall Banner

by Jennifer Garry for We R Memory Keepers

Autumn is a beautiful time of the year... fall leaves rustle.

MATERIALS:
Paper Accents chipboard pennants (2-Point: four 5" x 8") • *We R Memory Keepers* Autumn Splendor decorative papers • Die cuts (letters, ovals, leaf shapes) • Rhinestone stickers • Buttons & floss to tie to the buttons • Brads • Twine • Ribbon (Orange, Brown, Teal) • Pop Dots adhesive • White glue

INSTRUCTIONS - size 8" x 27":
Add embellishments to each pennant. Tie pennants together with twine. Tie tulle ribbon bows to twine between the pennants.

Gratitude Banner

by Donna Goss

An attitude of gratitude is the key to a happy life. This banner would be wonderful at a retirement party or in recognition of generous deeds.

MATERIALS:
Paper Accents chipboard pennants (2-Point: nine 5" x 8", one 4" x 6") • Solid color cardstock (Orange, Dark Green, Cream) • Decorative cardstock • Brown bubble letter stickers • 21 puffy glitter leaves • 12 paper flowers • 3 yards Gold glitter tape • 4 yards *Zipperstop* Leather Tan seam binding • *Ranger* (Aged Mohagony Distress pad, Adirondack Gold paint dabber, Ink blending tool, Cranberry Colorwash spray) • 18 Copper $\frac{3}{16}$" eyelets • *Spellbinder* Nestabilities $2\frac{3}{8}$" circle die • 3" scallop circle punch • *We R Memory Keepers* Crop-a-dile • Pencil • Scissors • Pop Dots • Hot glue gun • Hot glue • PVA glue and glue brush

INSTRUCTIONS - size 8" x 55":
Paint back and edges of pennants using dabber. Let dry. Cover pennants with papers and ink the edges with Aged Mohagony. Apply glitter tape to top edges of small pennants. Glue small pennants to large. Punch holes at top of large pennants and set eyelets. Punch 9 cardstock 3" scallop circles and attach to small pennants with foam dots. Die cut 9 cardstock $2\frac{3}{8}$" circles and ink the edges. Apply sticker letters. Spray paper flowers with Colorwash and let dry. Hot glue leaves and flowers to pennants. Tie pennants together with 12" ribbons. Knot securely. Tie 20" ribbons to outside eyelets on first and last pennants. Knot securely.

Faith

by Aldean Tendick

Reassuring colors blend elegantly with lacy borders and rhinestones.

MATERIALS:
Paper Accents chipboard pennants (Triangle: five 6" x 9") • Velvet paper (White, Tan, Light Brown) • Decorative papers • *Martha Stewart* Lace Doily punch • Die cut machine, dies for 4" tall letters and flourishes • Gem, rhinestone and pearl stickers • 2 yards Brown satin $\frac{1}{4}$" wide ribbon • Light Brown chalk ink • Hole punch • Mini Glue Dots • Tape runner

INSTRUCTIONS - size 9" x 32":
Die cut letters and flourishes from Tan and Light Brown velvet paper. Punch lace borders from White velvet paper. Cover pennants with paper. Ink the edges. Adhere letters and embellishments. Punch holes in pennants. String pennants together with ribbon, tying bows between each pennant. Secure bows in place.

Give Thanks

by Aldean Tendick

In 1863, President Lincoln declared a national day of Thanksgiving. Today, we continue the tradition, kicking off the winter holiday season with a day of thanks.

MATERIALS:
Paper Accents chipboard pennants (2-Point: ten 5" x 8")
• Textured cardstock in fall colors • Decorative paper • Autumn motif stickers & die cuts • Die cut letters 3½" tall • 3 yards Tan raffia ribbon • Dew drops • *Sakura* Black Micron .05 pen • White glue • Tape

INSTRUCTIONS - size 8" x 75":
Cover chipboard shapes with papers. Pen-stitch around the edge of each pennant. Adhere letters and embellishments. Tie pennants together with raffia.

Boo to You!

by Donna Goss

Happy Haunting! Nothing makes a Halloween party a treat like boo-tiful decorations in bewitching seasonal motifs.

MATERIALS:
Paper Accents chipboard pennants (2-Point: three 4" x 6") • Decorative cardstock • 2 yards Orange ½" wide rickrack • 2 yards *Zipperstop* Black ½" wide seam binding • 10" Black ⅛" wide satin ribbon • 2 felt spiders • 1 Black tulle Halloween bat • Glittered dot embellishments (6 small Orange, 6 large Black) • Chipboard letters 2½" tall • 7 Black ³⁄₁₆" eyelets • *Ranger* (Adirondack Pitch Black paint dabber, Ink blending tool, Orange Peel Stickles, Enamel accents, ⅛" Wonder tape) • *We R*

Memory Keepers Crop-a-dile • Paint brush • Pencil • Scissors • The Ultimate! glue • PVA glue and glue brush

INSTRUCTIONS - size 8" x 14":
Paint back and edges of pennants using dabber. Let dry. Cover pennants with papers. Tape rickrack to pennant edges. Punch 2 holes in each pennant at top and 1 hole in center bottom of middle pennant and set eyelets. Paint letters with dabber and use paint brush to get into small areas. Let dry. Tape a letter to each pennant. Glue dot embellishments and felt spiders in place. Hang bat from eyelet in middle pennant using the Black ribbon. Apply Stickles to the spiders.
Apply enamel to the letters straight from bottle. Outline letter first and then fill in. Turn bottle upside down and squeeze to apply keeping pressure on bottle to prevent bubbles. Product is self leveling and dries to a glossy finish. Tie pennants together with 12" ribbons. Knot securely.
Tie 20" ribbons to outside eyelets on first and last pennants. Knot securely.

Apply Enamel to Letters
Apply enamel straight from bottle. Outline letter first then fill in between the outlines.

Boo Banner

by Terry Olson

I love the paper on this banner - "The Apothecary Emporium - Bat wings to be used by certified wizards only" What fun!

MATERIALS:
Paper Accents chipboard pennants (2-Point: one 10" x 16") • Decorative papers • Red glitter paint • 1 yard Black ribbon • Rhinestone glue strips • 2 plastic bead dangles • Silk flower • Pin back • Pop Dots adhesive • White glue

INSTRUCTIONS - size 10" x 16" (not including hanger):
Cover chipboard shape with papers. Cut a cardstock oval and cover with paper. Adhere oval to center with Pop Dots. Paint "Boo" and splatters with glitter paint. Adhere rhinestones to edges. Attach rhinestone dangles to pennant points. Run ribbon through holes, center and knot the ends. Attach pin back to back of flower. Pin flower to center of ribbon.

Treat Cones

by Terry Olson

Offer guest treats in three sizes and hang them within easy reach.

MATERIALS:
Paper Accents chipboard pennants (Triangle: three 6" x 9", three 4" x 6", three mini 2¾" x 4") • Decorative papers • Ribbon 3 yards each (Black, Twill) • Rhinestone glue strips • Plastic bead dangle • Double sided tape • White glue

INSTRUCTIONS:

sizes 6" x 9", 4" x 6", 2¾" x 4"
    (not including hanger)
Cover chipboard shapes with papers. Form a triangular cone and tape inside. String ribbon through the corners. Adhere rhinestones to edges. Attach rhinestone dangles to point of large cone. Run ribbon through holes, center and knot the ends. Tie a twill ribbon bow to the center of the hanger ribbon.

Spooky Banner

by Mona Johnson for Bazzill Basics

Your house will be the favorite haunt of everyone in the neighborhood when you hang up this banner inviting all to enter for an enchanting evening of bewitching fun.

MATERIALS:
Paper Accents chipboard pennants (ten 8" x 12") • *Bazzill Basics* Black paper and colored papers • Halloween embellishments & die cut paper shapes • ⅛ yard tulle (Black, Orange, Lime Green) • Rhinestone glue strips & gem stickers • Paper flowers • Brads • Letter stamps and ink pad • Pop Dots adhesive • White glue

INSTRUCTIONS - size 12" x 58":
Cover chipboard shapes with Black paper. Add embellishments to each pennant. Cut tulle into strips. Tie pennants together with tulle.

Kites Flying in the Breeze

by Linda Kretz for My Little Shoebox

*Let's go fly a kite, up to the highest height. Let's go fly a kite and send it soaring...
Here's a project that captures the joy of one of life's simplest pleasures.*

MATERIALS:

Paper Accents chipboard pennants (Scallop Triangle: ten 6" x 9", four 12" x 12") • Decorative papers • Die cut embellishments • 1 yard Brown $1/2$" wide rickrack • Assorted ribbon bows • Lace with button fringe • Paper flowers • Scraps of ribbon and lace • 5 yards each of 2 sheer ribbons • Plastic drinking straw • White paint • Paint brush • Glitter glue • $1/4$" hole punch • Glue gun • Hot glue • Double sided tape • *Ranger* Inkssentials Pop It Shapes • Scissors

INSTRUCTIONS - size 14" x 65":

Cut $61/2$" x 8" kite shapes from 12" chipboard. Cover kites with papers and embellish as desired.

Cloud Embellishments: Cut 2 large and 2 small cloud shapes from chipboard. Paint all White. Let dry. Cover with glitter glue. Let dry. Hot glue a piece of straw onto the back of the large cloud. Attach a small cloud to the front with Pop Dots shapes. Cover pennants with paper. Punch holes. Attach decorated kites with Pop It Shapes. Tie pennants together with sheer ribbon. Thread a cloud embellishment on each end of the ribbon, passing the ribbon through the straw.

Cloud Embellishments

1. Cut cloud shapes from White cardstock. Add pearlescent glitter.

2. Adhere 2 or 3 cloud shapes together in layers with Pop Dots. Glue a straw to the back.

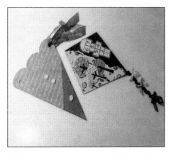

3. Thread ribbons through holes in Scallop Triangles. Adhere a kite to each pennant with Pop Dots.

Sweetheart Love Banner

by Donna Goss

Love is in the air all year long, so you'll get a lot of use from this pretty banner. Hearts are a wonderful motif for celebrations that range from a romantic dinner for two to your 50th wedding anniversary. This will be lovely at Valentine's Day too.

MATERIALS:

Paper Accents chipboard pennants (Arched: four 5" x 8") • Decorative papers • $21/2$ yards White $1/8$" wide rickrack • 8 heart shaped $1/4$" eyelets • 2 yards Pink sheer $3/4$" wide ribbon • 2 glittered 6" Pink foam hearts • 2 Pink plain 6" foam hearts • 4 heart 4" doilies • *Zipperstop* White seam binding ribbon (three $1/2$" x 10", two $1/2$" x 20") • 40" Pink tulle fringe trim • 4 decorative cardstock strips $21/2$" x 11" • 4 book page strips $21/2$" x 11" • White cardstock (twelve 1" circles, four $21/2$" x $21/2$" squares) • *Ranger* (Jet Black archival ink, $1/8$" Wonder tape) • *Hero Arts* LOVE alphabet letter stamps • *Sizzix* die cut machine, rosette die • $1/4$" hole punch • Eyelet tools • Hot glue gun • Hot glue • White glue • Scissors

INSTRUCTIONS - size 8" x 30":

Cover pennants with paper. Trim the edge of each pennant with rickrack. Cut 4 paper strips $21/2$" x 5", fold in half and tape to the top front of each pennant. Turn the pennant over and punch holes in the top of each pennant. Fold down the flap and tape in place. Punch holes. Set eyelets. String pennants together with Pink sheer ribbon.

Rosettes - Die cut 4 rosettes each from cardstock and book page strips. Accordion fold them and tape ends together. Hot glue cardstock circles to both the front and back of the cardstock rosettes. Hot glue circles to the backs only of the book page rosettes. Die cut spiked circles from White squares. Stamp letters on spiked circles in Black ink. Hot glue them to the fronts of the book page rosettes. Hot glue heart doilies to foam hearts. Hot glue cardstock rosettes to the book page ones. Glue Pink tulle fringe to back of cardstock rosettes.

Hot glue layers to heart doilies. Punch holes in foam hearts. Tie hearts together with 10" pieces of seam binding or ribbon. Thread 20" pieces of seam binding to outside holes of L & E hearts for hanging. Knot securely. Glue heart banner to pennant banner.